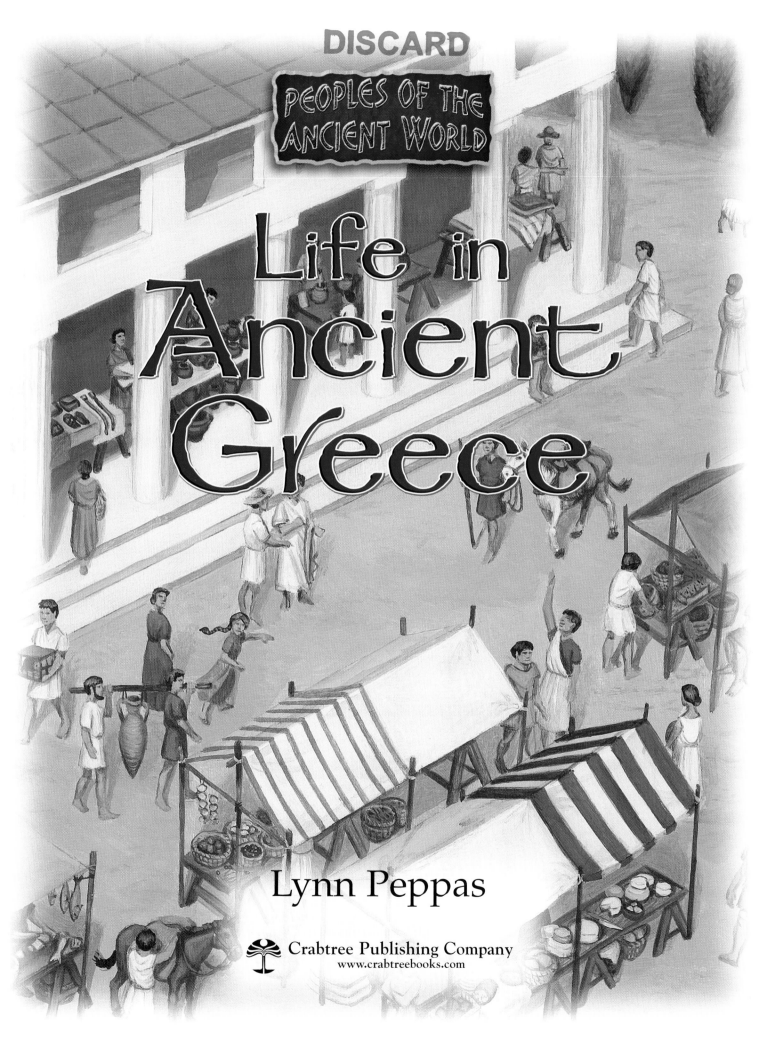

PEOPLES OF THE ANCIENT WORLD

Life in Ancient Greece

Lynn Peppas

Crabtree Publishing Company
www.crabtreebooks.com

Crabtree Publishing Company

www.crabtreebooks.com

For Neil MacIntyre

Coordinating editor: Ellen Rodger
Project editor: Sean Charlebois
Editors: Rachel Eagen, Carrie Gleason, Adrianna Morganelli
Production coordinator: Rosie Gowsell
Production assistance: Samara Parent
Scanning technician: Arlene Arch-Wilson
Photo research: Allison Napier
Art director: Rob MacGregor

Project management assistance:
Media Projects, Inc.
Carter Smith
Pat Smith
Laura Smyth
Aimee Kraus
Michael Greenhut

Consultants: Dr. Anton Jansen, Department of Classics, Brock University; Barbara Richman, Farragut Middle School, Hastings-on-Hudson, New York

Photographs: Alinari / Art Resource, NY: p. 23 (bottom); American School of Classical Studies, Athens: p. 10 (bottom); Archivo Iconografico, S.A./CORBIS: p. 8; Bettmann/CORBIS: p. 8 (bottom), p. 9, p. 30; Bildarchiv Preussischer Kulturbesitz / Art Resource, NY: p. 25 (top); Lawrence Gresswell; Eye Ubiquitous/CORBIS: p. 29; Robert Gill; Papilio/CORBIS: p. 7; Wolfgang Kaehler/CORBIS: p. 3, pp. 4–5; Erich Lessing / Art Resource, NY: p. 22 (top); p. 28, p. 31; Nimatallah/Art Resource, NY: p. 24, p. 26; Réunion des Musées Nationaux / Art Resource, NY: p. 22 (bottom); Scala / Art Resource, NY: p. 26 (bottom), p. 27; Vanni Archive / CORBIS: p. 7; Jim Winkley; Ecoscene/CORBIS: p. 23 (top).

Illustrations: James Burmester: p. 28 (columns); Jeff Crosby: p. 1; Lorne Fast: p. 11 (Hoplite); Roman Goforth: p. 10 (top), pp. 14–15, p. 24; Rose Gowsell (Minotour), p. 5, p. 28; Robert McGregor: p. 3 (timeline), p. 6 (map), p. 7 (boat), p. 25 (athlete); Ole Skedsmo: p. 15, p. 16, p. 17

Cartography: Jim Chernishenko: p. 6

Cover: Close up view of The Charioteer of Delphi, an ancient Greek statue.

Contents: The Temple of Apollo in modern Greece has survived for centuries.

Title page: Shoppers and merchants gather to buy and sell goods and produce at the Athens Agora, or main market.

Crabtree Publishing Company

www.crabtreebooks.com   1-800-387-7650

Cataloging-in-Publication data
Peppas, Lynn.
  Life in ancient Greece / written by Lynn Peppas.
    p. cm. -- (Peoples of the ancient world)
  Includes index.
   ISBN 0-7787-2035-7 (rlb) -- ISBN 0-7787-2065-9 (pbk)
  1. Greece--Civilization--To 146 B.C.--Juvenile literature. I. Title.
  II. Series.
   DF77.P39 2004
   938--dc22
                                        2004013065
                                          LC

Published in the United States
PMB 16A
350 Fifth Ave.
Suite 3308
New York, NY
10118

Published in Canada
616 Welland Ave.
St. Catharines
Ontario, Canada
L2M 5V6

Published in the United Kingdom
73 Lime Walk
Headington
Oxford
0X3 7AD
United Kingdom

Published in Australia
386 Mt. Alexander Rd.
Ascot Vale (Melbourne)
V1C 3032

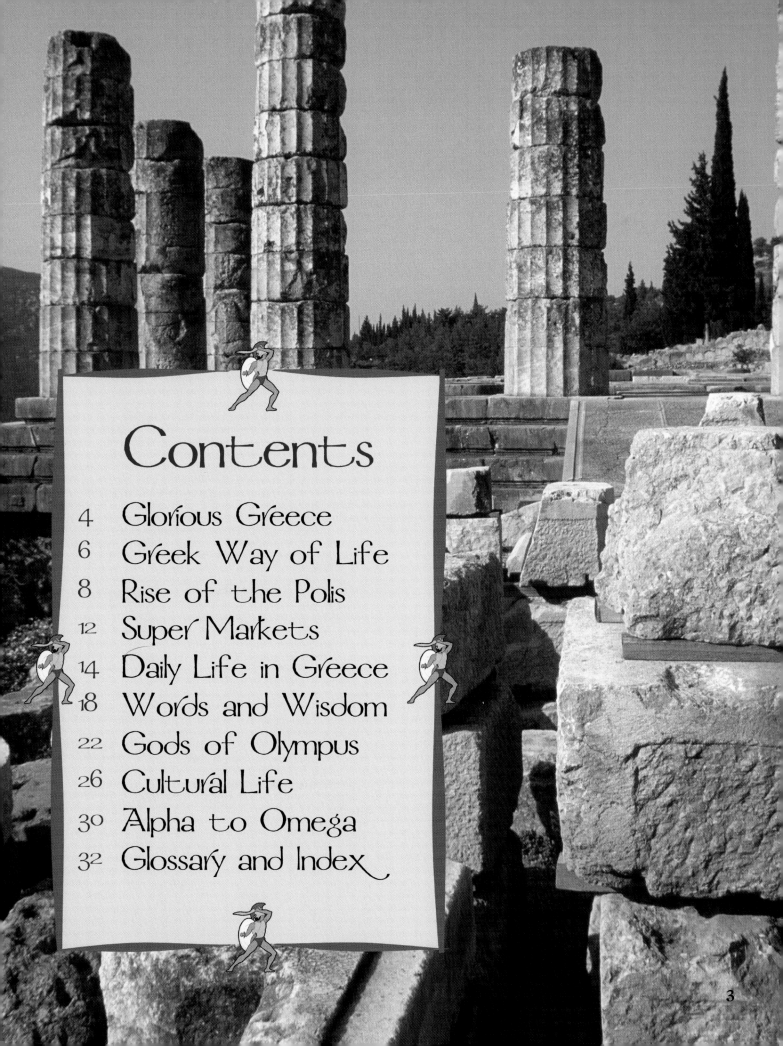

Contents

Glorious Greece

According to legend, the early Greeks were a race of heroes. They sailed the seas in search of a golden sheepskin, fought a ten-year war over the love of a beautiful woman, and slayed snake-haired monsters, all to prove themselves to their gods. Although most of this is fiction, certain details were based on fact. The real-life Greek people made some of the greatest achievements in history.

Ancient Greek civilization flourished from 1800 B.C. to 150 B.C. Small independent communities, called city-states, rose up throughout the Greek world. The rugged landscape meant that food production and travel between city-states was difficult, yet the hardships made the ancient Greeks a tough people who left the world an amazing legacy of art and architecture, poetry and drama, philosophy and science. The Greeks gave the world democracy, a form of government born in Athens, and belief in the worth of individual people.

Bronze Age

3000 B.C. - 1200 B.C.

▸ *The Minoans create the first Greek civilization around 2200 B.C.*

Dark Age

1200 B.C. - 800 B.C.

◂ *The Trojan War is fought between Greece and Troy around 1200 B.C.*

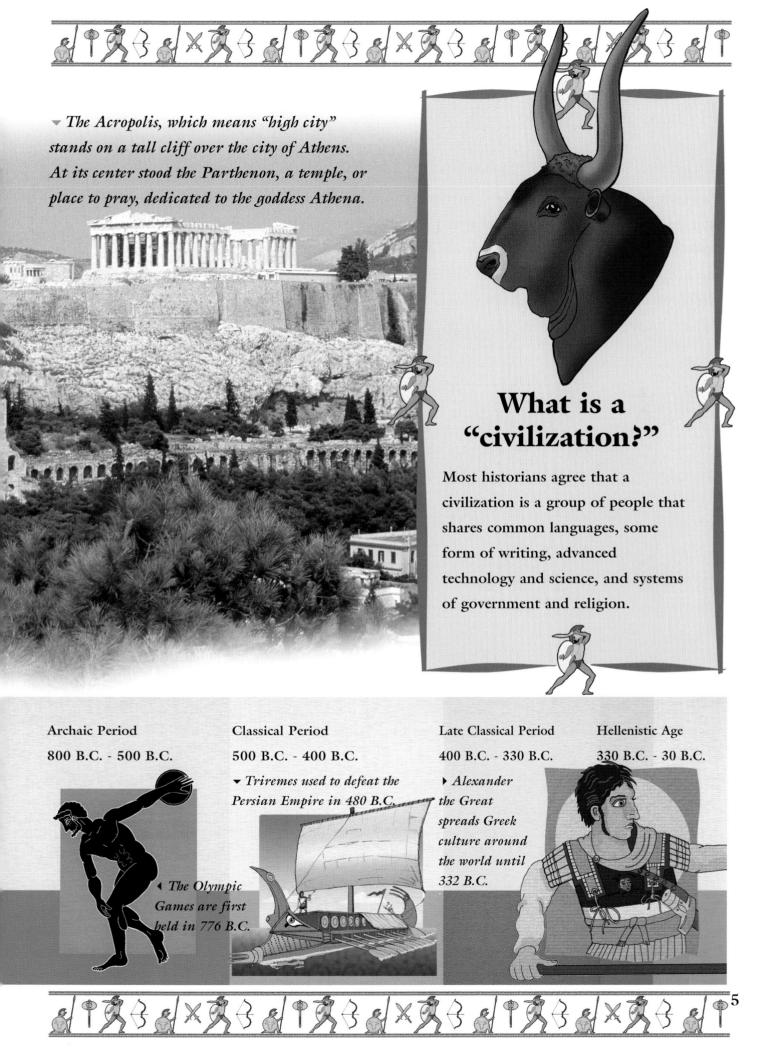

The Acropolis, which means "high city" stands on a tall cliff over the city of Athens. At its center stood the Parthenon, a temple, or place to pray, dedicated to the goddess Athena.

What is a "civilization?"

Most historians agree that a civilization is a group of people that shares common languages, some form of writing, advanced technology and science, and systems of government and religion.

Archaic Period
800 B.C. - 500 B.C.

The Olympic Games are first held in 776 B.C.

Classical Period
500 B.C. - 400 B.C.

Triremes used to defeat the Persian Empire in 480 B.C.

Late Classical Period
400 B.C. - 330 B.C.

Alexander the Great spreads Greek culture around the world until 332 B.C.

Hellenistic Age
330 B.C. - 30 B.C.

Greek Way of Life

Ancient Greece was not one country. It was a group of individual communities scattered along the rugged landscape of the Greek mainland and on about 170 islands in the Aegean Sea. Each community was separated from the next by either mountains or sea. The ancient Greeks developed a way of life that was inspired by their land, becoming expert sailors, traders, and warriors.

A Rocky Land

Mainland Greece is a **peninsula** that stretches out into the Mediterranean Sea. The northeast part of Greece, where the city of Athens is located, is called Attica. The southern tip, where Sparta is found, is called the Peloponnese. Ancient Greece had many mountainous islands, as well as **colonies** around the Mediterranean Sea in Sicily, North Africa, and Asia Minor, which is now Turkey. Other ancient peoples surrounded the Greeks, including the Egyptians in the south, the Persians in the east, and the Thracians in the north.

▲ *Greece's rocky soil and location on the Mediterranean Sea were the main reasons why the Greeks founded many colonies overseas. The Greeks used the word Hellas to describe places where they established a Greek way of life.*

A Harsh Land

Mountains and barren plains covered most of Greece so farmers struggled hard to produce crops. Only one quarter of Greece's land was arable, or suitable for farming. Pockets of soil between the mountains were deep and level and farmers there grew grain, grapes for wine, and olive groves. Farmers learned how to drain swamps and **terrace** hillsides. Fields were often left unplanted for a season so the land could recover and be **replenished**. Lack of farmland was the main reason why Greeks established colonies around the Mediterranean Sea.

Resources

The forests of northern Greece provided timber to the south where wood was scarce. Greece's rocky land provided **minerals** for tools and weapons, and marble and stone for buildings and sculptures. Mines near Athens were rich in silver, marble, iron, and lead. Slaves were forced to work these mines day and night for merchants to trade these precious items around the world.

Call of the Sea

Most ancient Greek cities were built near the coast so shipping and fishing were easy. The Greeks panned the sea for salt and fishers caught tuna fish, anchovies, and sardines. When a city did not have enough food, people moved to colonies. Colonies were useful trading posts for merchants to trade goods they produced, such as olive oil and minerals, for wheat, wood, and other items they needed.

▲ *The ancient Greeks believed mountains were made by gods living on top of Mount Olympus.*
◄ *The people of Greece built ships called triremes that carried them to new lands to live, trade, and fight wars.*

Rise of the Polis

The earliest peoples of Greece were the Minoans and the Mycenaeans. Around 800 B.C., independent city-states, such as Athens and Sparta, rose up across the Greek mainland.

Minoans and Mycenaeans

The Minoans built the first great Greek civilization on the island of Crete in the Mediterranean Sea between 2200 B.C. and 1400 B.C. Around 1580 B.C., a war-like people settled in a coastal city in the southern Peloponnese called Mycenae. The Mycenaneans ruled Greece for 400 years before their civilization collapsed. The end of the Mycenanean civilization plunged Greece into a period called the Dark Ages, which lasted until 800 B.C.

From Tyranny to Democracy

Around 800 B.C., the Greek people began founding a number of small, independent city-states. Each city-state, or *polis*, controlled the villages and farmland around it and had its own laws, government, and system of money. At first, all city-states were ruled by a *basileus*, or king. Most kings were overthrown by the people and replaced with oligarchies.

Oligarchies were governments where only a few wealthy citizens ruled. In some city-states, tyrants came to power by overthrowing the kings or oligarchies. Tyrants were men who held onto power by military force and fear. Some tyrants ruled for years, but over time people began to favor oligarchy or democracy, a government led by the free, male citizens of the city-state.

▲ *According to Greek legend, Mycenae was ruled by King Agamemnon. For many years it was believed this burial mask belonged to Agamemnon.*

◂ *Pericles (center) was a general elected by the Athenian people fourteen times. Pericles undertook many large building projects, such as the Acropolis.*

Sparta

The city-state of Sparta was founded in 950 B.C. and organized as a military camp. Over time, Sparta conquered almost all the surrounding lands in the Peloponnese, using the land for farming and forcing the conquered people into slavery. Spartans were heavily outnumbered by their slaves and servants and so needed to rule by fear. Slaves in Sparta were called *helots* and they were forced to do all the heavy work while Spartan men dedicated themselves to war. Sparta was ruled by an oligarchy of two military generals. The generals made all the decisions and ordinary citizens had no power.

▲ *Sparta was a city-state that was almost constantly at war or preparing for war.*

Athens

By the mid-400s B.C., Athens had grown into the most powerful city-state in Greece. Athens created a new form of government based on the rule of the people. It was called democracy, from the Greek word *demos*, meaning "the people." Every male citizen got a vote when it came to electing officials to run the city and make laws, but women and slaves were not allowed to vote. The main governing body was the assembly of all citizens, or *ecclesia*, which gathered 40 times a year on a hillside. In 508 B.C., the Athenian leader Cleisthenes guaranteed that free adult male citizens were automatically members of the *ecclesia*. In times of war, ten military generals called *strategoi* made decisions about defending the city.

Democracy in Action

In Athens, all citizens played a role in running the city-state. The *ecclesia* met in a hillside **amphitheater** that seated 18,000 people. All citizens could make a speech and vote at the *ecclesia*. A smaller group of people, called the *boule*, met daily to decide what important business the *ecclesia* would discuss and vote on. The *boule* was made up of 500 citizens who were chosen **randomly**. Laws that were passed by the *ecclesia* were upheld by the courts. Athenian courts had no judges or lawyers. An official kept order while a person accused of a crime defended himself. A **jury** of between 200 and 2,500 citizens was drawn from names in a bowl. The jury determined whether a person was guilty or not guilty.

▲ *The citizens of Athens voted for people to fill all important jobs, such as military generals. One method of voting was to drop a colored stone into a vase. Whoever had the most stones won the vote.*

Waging War

Fighting in a war was the supreme test of a Greek man. A city-state prospered if it had a strong navy to protect it from invaders such as the Persians, and from pirates of the Aegean Sea who preyed on its trading ships. In Athens, military generals were elected and every citizen could be called on to fight. At age eighteen, Athenian men from wealthy families went for two years of training for war. Open spaces around the *gymnasia*, or schools for physical education, were used to train the Athenian **cavalry** and army.

◄ *During a trial, jurors were given two ballots. A ballot with a hollow post (top left) meant guilty and one with a solid post meant not-guilty.*

Arming a Hoplite

Most Greek battles were fought between small armies. During battle, the most successful foot soldier was the hoplite. A hoplite was an amored spear carrier, who took his name from the large circular shield, called a hoplon, which he carried. A hoplite was usually a wealthy citizen because he had to supply his own weapons and armor.

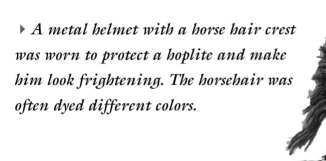

▶ *A metal helmet with a horse hair crest was worn to protect a hoplite and make him look frightening. The horsehair was often dyed different colors.*

▶ *Around his torso, a hoplite wore bronze body armor called a cuirass. Each hoplite had his cuirass made to fit him especially.*

▼ *A hoplite carried a heavy round shield called a hoplon. A hoplon was wooden with a bronze rim. It was carried in a hoplite's left hand.*

▲ *Each hoplite decorated his shield with a personalized emblem.*

▲ *A hoplite sometimes carried a short sword, but his main weapon was a thrusting spear about seven feet (two meters) long.*

◀ *On each leg, a hoplite wore bronze shin guards called greaves.*

Super Markets

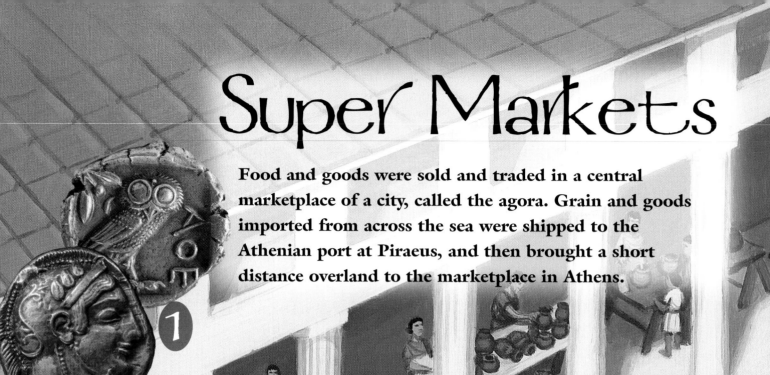

Food and goods were sold and traded in a central marketplace of a city, called the agora. Grain and goods imported from across the sea were shipped to the Athenian port at Piraeus, and then brought a short distance overland to the marketplace in Athens.

1. After 500 B.C., most city-states had their own gold or silver coins, and decorated them with local gods or symbols. The silver Athenian coin displayed the goddess Athena on one side and an eagle on the other.

2. The agora was an important place in all Greek cities. Local **artisans** kept their workshops near the agora to attract shoppers.

3. The agora's central location within the city also made it a place where men could meet and discuss ideas and politics.

4. Local farmers and vendors hauled their wares in carts they pulled themselves or with a donkey.

5. The agora was like a modern day shopping mall that sold items such as food, clothing, housewares, pottery, and slaves.

6. Women could draw water from a well lcoated in the agora.

Ancient Greek society depended on people doing different tasks. The wealthy lived a life of leisure, often serving in politics or debating philosophy. Many people were farmers, while others were teachers, merchants, sailors, metal workers, and marble workers. Most hard labor was done by slaves.

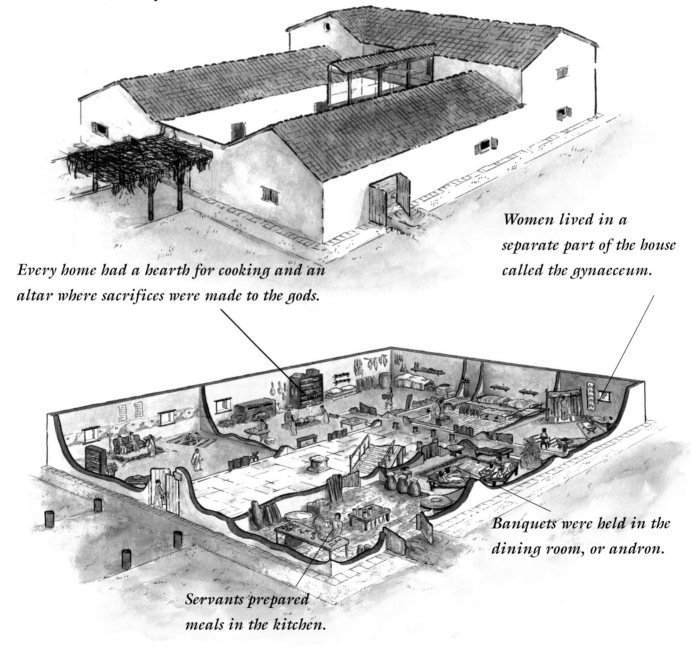

Every home had a hearth for cooking and an altar where sacrifices were made to the gods.

Women lived in a separate part of the house called the gynaeceum.

Banquets were held in the dining room, or andron.

Servants prepared meals in the kitchen.

Home Greek Home

Within a city's walls, homes were crowded close together. The homes were one story, with painted mud-brick walls set on stone foundations. Flat roofs provided a place where families gathered in the cool of the evening. Windows were high and had wooden shutters to give privacy from the bustle in the streets. Wealthy Greeks lived in two-story homes that looked inward over an open courtyard. No central heating was needed in Greece's warm climate. Some rooms had beautiful **mosaic** floors and **frescoed** walls, where scenes of gods and everyday life were painted onto the wet plaster. Carved chests, tables, couches, and three-legged chairs provided comfort, and carpets and curtains added more color. Homes did not have a private bath or well. People got water at the public fountain at the agora.

Slaves and Metics

In Athens, slaves did the backbreaking work. Slaves were abandoned infants, prisoners of war, criminals, or individuals bought at market from the slave traders. Slaves could not raise their own children, but they were not taxed or forced into military service. A freedman was a slave who earned his freedom by buying it from his master. Other manual laborers were metics. Metics were foreigners, or people from other places. Sometimes metics became wealthy saving the money they earned. Metics could not vote, marry an Athenian citizen, or own property in Athens. Metics still had to pay taxes and do military service.

▶ *Household servants filled pottery jugs with water for their masters. Some homes had wells, but most servants got the water at the agora.*

Women's Quiet Lives

A woman's role in ancient Greek society depended on whether she was married and in which city-state she lived. A married woman in Athens stayed home, in separate quarters, away from the windows. She could go out in public for a special occasion, such as a funeral, religious festival, or family visit, as long as she was accompanied by a member of her household. It was her job to raise children, spin wool and **flax**, and weave it into bedding and clothes. She had to manage servants or slaves and care for them when they were ill. Athenian women could not vote, own land, or participate in business. In the city-state of Sparta, women could own property and manage it. Women were not formally educated, but some women could read and write. Often, a girl left home at about age fifteen, for married life with a much older man who was chosen by her father.

◄ *Women wore a long garment called a* **peplos,** *held on by brooches and worn with a belt.*

Here Comes the Bride

Marriage in ancient Greece was a business deal between the parents of the bride and groom. A girl's father offered the groom a dowry, which consisted of money, clothing, jewelry, animals, or slaves. If he accepted, the wedding was arranged. Before the wedding, a bride had a ceremonial bath and put on bright clothes and a veil. The wedding began with an all-day feast at the bride's home. Then the groom led the bride to his family's house, with guests holding torches to light the darkened streets and musicians playing flutes and lyres. The newlyweds ate wedding cake made from sesame seeds and honey. The act of sharing food in her husband's home sealed the marriage bond.

▶ *Before the wedding, a bride sacrificed her toys of childhood to the goddess Artemis and asked her blessing for the marriage.*

Clothing

Clothing in ancient Greece consisted of a loose-fitting tunic. A cloak was worn in cooler weather and on special occasions. In times of peace and prosperity, fashions of the wealthy were showy and colorful. During war, fancy dress was not worn. Around 550 B.C., the *chiton* became popular. The chiton was a linen garment imported from the east that men and women wore. Wealthy Greeks wore leather sandals, although many people went barefoot in the summer. Wealthy men and women wore their hair long. Women wore elaborate hairstyles kept in place with ribbons or hairnets. Some women wore wigs. Men fastened their hair up with a gold brooch. Greek men grew beards and women used makeup made from plants to redden their cheeks and whiten their skin.

▸ *Simple, loose-fitting clothes allowed freedom of movement for men. The outer garment is called a* **himation**.

himation

chiton

sandals

▾ *Olive trees were grown by many Greek families. Olives were an important part of Greek life. Olive oil was spread on bread like butter and used as a cleanser like soap.*

What's On the Menu?

Poorer families in ancient Greece ate barley cakes, called *maza*, and enjoyed meat only during festivals. When times were good, they added goat's cheese, olives, salted fish, **legumes**, and vegetables to the menu. The wealthy ate lamb, goat, pig, or dog every day. They drank wine, and had bread baked from grains such as wheat or barley. Flatbreads, such as pita, were used as an edible **utensil** to pick up food cooked in sauces. The seas provided fish and seafood. Poorer people ate salted and dried fish, while the wealthy ate shark meat, eel, and octopus.

Words and Wisdom

The ancient Greeks developed their own language and system of numbers. The physical world excited the curiosity of the Greeks and they became the founders of mathematics, science, and philosophy.

School Days

Education was for the sons of wealthy Athenian families only. Boys started school at age seven and were taught to read and write, recite poetry from memory, and to play a musical instrument such as the lyre or flute. Education also included wrestling, boxing, running, and throwing a javelin and discus. Sports encouraged the competitive spirit and prepared young men to enter one of Greece's most popular sporting events, the Olympics. Girls in Athens did not go to school. They stayed home and learned spinning and weaving from their mothers. Some wealthy families hired private tutors who taught girls to read and write. In Sparta, girls trained to be strong so they could give birth to healthy babies who would grow up to be great soldiers.

▼ Wealthy boys from Athens were taken to their lessons by a slave called a paidogogus, who is sitting behind the pupil in this vase painting.

A Universal Language

By about 1500 B.C., Greek-speaking people were established in Greece, probably having come as invaders from the north. There were a number of **dialects** of the Greek language, the most important of which were Attic, Doric, and Ionic. Ancient Greek was spoken on the Greek mainland, the Greek islands, Asia Minor, Italy, and Sicily. The political and cultural power of Athens made the Athenian dialect, Attic, the most spoken. From the Attic dialect there developed a version called the *koine* which means "common" or "common to all the people." Koine became the standard form of ancient Greek.

When the Greeks began conquering other people and colonizing other lands, koine became a common language. Koine was an important language in the Mediterranean and parts of Asia Minor and Africa for many centuries.

◄ *Pythagoras was a Greek scholar who started a school for boys and girls to study music, astronomy, and arithmetic. Pythagorus developed methods of doing math that are still used today.*

Greece is the Word

The English word "alphabet" comes from the first two letters in the Greek alphabet, "alpha" and "beta." In 700 B.C., the Greeks adapted their alphabet from their neighbors, the Phoenicians.

By 500 B.C., the Greeks made the Phoenician alphabet their own by adding five vowels and writing from left to right, as we do, and not right to left, as the Phoenicians did. The Greek alphabet has changed little since ancient times.

GREEK WORDS (English Translation)	ANCIENT GREEK MEANING	ENGLISH WORD
ΑΚΑΔΗΜΙΑ (akademeia)	The Academy	Academy
ΔΥΝΑΜΙΚΟΣ (dynamikos)	Powerful	Dynamic
ΠΟΙΗΤΗΣ (poietes)	Creator, poet	Poet
ΣΧΟΛΗ (schole)	Free time, leisure, discussion	School

Great Thinkers

The ancient Greeks were interested in learning the truth about human behavior. Thinkers known as philosophers studied why people act the way they do. The best known Greek philosophers were Socrates, Plato, and Aristotle. Socrates was interested in ethics, or the nature of right and wrong. He taught students to question everything to get at the truth. Socrates even questioned the wisdom of Athenian democracy, arguing that not every citizen should be allowed to govern. This made Athenian rulers angry, and in 399 B.C. they had him executed. Some Greek philosophers were scientists who studied plants and animals. In 335 B.C., Socrates' student, Plato, founded a school and library called the Academy, outside Athens. Plato believed that many things that could not be seen, such as human goodness, existed in the world.

▲ *Aristotle was a greek philosopher who wrote about nature, science, math, and politics. He was known to walk about as he lectured and once worked as a tutor to Alexander the Great, who later conquered most of the world.*

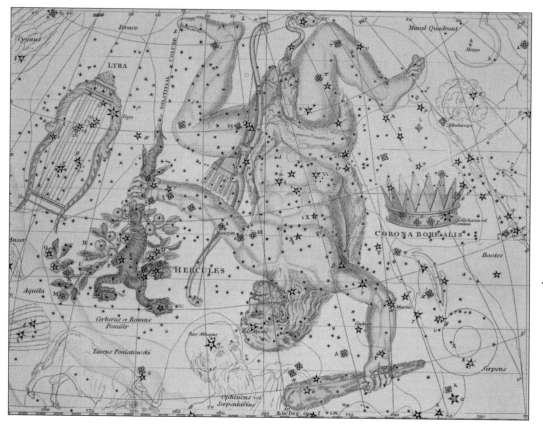

◄ *The ancient Greeks used the study of the stars, or astronomy, for navigating the seas and for marking the days, months, and years.*

Healing Arts

Sick people in ancient Greece relied on magic charms to cure them. They flocked to shrines to make offerings to the gods, in the hope of getting relief from ailments such as headaches, blindness, and pimples. Ancient Greek doctors healed wounds caused by war and fractures and dislocations common with athletes but they knew very little about disease. Ancient Greek medicine changed with the work of Hippocrates. Born on the island of Kos around 460 B.C., Hippocrates believed that time, not temple sacrifices, cured disease. He also believed that disease came from natural causes, not the actions of the gods. In order to avoid disease, people had to have good hygiene and eat a healthy diet. By considering the facts and then deciding what the sufferer had, Hippocrates predicted how a disease would progress.

▲ *Doctors today still take the Hippocratic Oath, which Hippocrates wrote. The oath says, "Whatever house I enter, I shall come to heal."*

Eureka!

The ancient Greeks were clever inventors. They invented the boat anchor and the catapult, which was used in war to hurl rocks at the enemy. The most famous Greek inventor was Archimedes and many of his inventions are still used today. One invention was a mechanical device known as Archimedes' screw. A screw is placed in a long cylinder. When the lower end of the cylinder is placed in water and the screw is turned, water is carried up through the cylinder to the top. Archimedes' screw was used to empty water from boats and to water crops.

▲ *An Archimedes' screw is a tool that is still used for irrigation in the Nile River delta in Egypt.*

Gods of Olympus

The ancient Greeks believed that their world was ruled by gods and goddesses. They created myths, or stories about the lives of gods, goddesses, and heroes. Heroes were special human beings descended from the gods.

Gods and Goddesses

The ancient Greeks believed that their gods and goddesses looked like muscular men and beautiful women but possessed **supernatural** powers. Gods could use the forces of nature to cause storms at sea, **famine**, or earthquakes. The most important gods and goddesses, such as Zeus, Athena, Poseidon, and Apollo were believd to live on top of Mount Olympus in northern Greece. Zeus, the king of the gods, ruled the sky and the weather. Athena was the goddess of wisdom. Posiedon ruled the sea and was the favorite god of the sailors. Apollo, god of the Sun, crossed the sky each day in his blazing chariot. The god Hades did not live on Mount Olympus but in the underworld where he judged people who died.

▲ *The Greeks had myths, or stories, about the origin of the Earth, as well as the origin of their gods. This painting depicts the myth of the birth of the goddess Athena. Athena was said to have sprung from Zeus' head in a full suit of armor.*

◄ *The ancient Greeks believed that when they died, their souls would be accompanied to the underworld by Hermes. Cerberus, the three-headed dog, guarded the gateway to the underworld.*

Heroic Stories

The Greeks also told stories about special human beings, descended from the gods, called heroes. The stories of these heroes often made points about human weaknesses and strength. Heracles was a great hero who accomplished many tasks that required enormous strength. Theseus was a hero who killed the dreaded Minotaur, a creature that was half man, half bull. Achilles is the greatest of all Greek heroes. During the **Trojan War** he fought bravely and defeated Troy's greatest warrior, Hector.

▲ *Every Greek city had a temple where the ancient Greek people came to worship, or honor, the god or goddess who protected the city.*

Reason for the Seasons

Ancient Greeks explained the weather, earthquakes, and disease with myths. The myth of Demeter and Persephone explains why the seasons change. When the goddess Demeter learned that Hades had kidnapped her daughter, Persephone, and taken the young girl to his underworld home to be his wife, she was filled with grief. When Demeter mourned her loss, nothing grew on the Earth. It became cold and barren and this was called winter. Zeus sent his messenger, Hermes, to rescue Persephone and return her to her mother. Demeter was so pleased that she brought new growth to the earth and this was called spring. Unfortunately, Persephone had to return to her husband in the underworld for a few months every year but came back to Mount Olympus and her mother every spring, starting the cycle of growth on Earth once again.

◀ *The ancient Greeks thought Demeter, the goddess of grain, caused things to grow.*

Religious Rituals and Sacrifice

The ancient Greeks believed that to please the gods they must worship them with elaborate festivals, athletic events, solemn rituals, and sacrifices. People offered the gods incense, flowers, pottery, gold, precious fabric, food, and wine. They believed that the gods also craved blood-sacrifice, so they killed animals, such as bulls, calves, sheep, boar, and pigs. An altar was first sprinkled with wine and barley and then the sacrificial victims were led to the altar where their throats were slit with a small knife or axe.

▲ *During religious festivals, lambs and other animals were sacrificed to the gods. When some animals, such as bulls, were sacrificed, they were decorated with garlands and ribbons.*

Religious Festivals

Religious festivals played an important part in ancient Greek life. Athenians celebrated the religious festival of Panathenaia every year. The Panathenaia honored Athena, the **patron** goddess of Athens, and thanked her for protecting the city. During this festival, the best musicians, athletes, and soldiers performed in competitions. A parade of twirling acrobats, singers, and costumed jugglers wound its way through the city to Athena's temple on the Acropolis. A massive statue of Athena was inside the Parthenon, in the shadowy **sanctuary**. It stood 40 feet (12 meters) tall and its wooden frame was covered with gold and ivory. Outside, at Athena's altar, 100 or more bulls were killed, roasted, and served to everyone. For the poor, the festival of Panathenaia was one of the few times they ate meat.

Oracles

Greeks who wanted to learn about what their future held consulted an oracle. An oracle was a god who gave answers to questions through a priestess. The most popular oracle was found at Delphi, where the sun god, Apollo, had a sanctuary. Apollo's advice was sought after by Greeks, foreigners, and even military generals. They all hoped the oracle would give them answers to specific questions, such as whether it was a good time to fight a war. Sometimes the oracle's advice was clear, while at other times it was confusing.

▶ *This painting from a vase shows a king receiving the answers of the oracle at Delphi from a priestess who is sitting on a three-legged seat called a tripod.*

Olympic Games

The ancient Olympic Games began in 776 B.C. in the town of Olympia as part of a religious festival to honor Zeus. The competition included wrestling, boxing, chariot racing, discus and javelin throwing, jumping, and running. The games brought together athletes, who competed naked, from all over Greece. During war, a truce brought a temporary end to fighting until the games were over. Champions were awarded garlands of olive leaves and ribbons to wear on their arms. Every city-state made its winning athletes into heroes and awarded them gifts when they returned home. Women could not compete in the games and married women were forbidden from even watching.

◀ *Throwing the discus, a flat bronze plate, was one sport in an Olympic event called the pentathalon, which means "five events."*

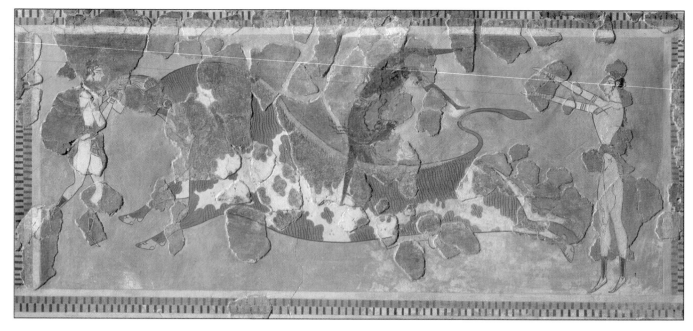

Cultural Life

The ancient Greeks believed their pottery, sculpture, and architecture needed to honor the gods. Poetry and plays told stories of exciting or tragic events that were influenced by the gods. Greek arts and culture reached their height in Athens from 500 B.C. to 400 B.C.

Pottery

The best pottery in ancient Greece came from Athens. Potters used a special local clay to make vases of many shapes and sizes in a reddish-brown color. These vases were used to carry, store, and mix water, wine, and olive oil. Vases were also traded widely around the Greek world. Before 530 B.C., vases were decorated with black figures on a red background. Later, red figures on a black background became popular.

▲ *Frescoes are made by applying colorful paint to wet* plaster *so that the color becomes fixed as the plaster dries. On the island of Crete, the Minoans decorated palaces and wealthy homes with frescoes.*

◄ *Greek vases, such as this* krater *used to mix wine and water, were painted with stories of Greek heroes, as well as scenes from daily life.*

Sculpture

Sculpture was an important part of the ancient Greek world. Early Greek sculptors admired and copied the statues of the ancient Egyptians, which they saw on trading voyages. The Greeks used a stone called white marble to create life-size statues known as *kourai* if they are male or *korai* if they are female. These statues were used to mark graves and to serve as memorials outside of temples. Later sculptors made more detailed sculptures of gods, statesmen, military heroes, athletes, and wealthy citizens. These statues were made of marble and were painted with vivid colors. Some statues were made of bronze. Statues often decorated public buildings and the homes of ordinary citizens.

▸ *Some Greek sculptures, such as this bronze of the god Zeus, show bodies in motion.*

Architecture

The greatest example of Greek architecture is the temple. A temple was usually built on a hill above the city from huge blocks of limestone and marble which were brought to the construction site by ox-cart. Stoneworkers called masons carved each block into its proper size. The temple's roof and ceiling were made of wood, and its roof tiles were made of **terra cotta**. Inside the temple, a room called the *naos* housed a large statue of a god or goddess. Only priests could enter the *naos*. This room was surrounded by rows of vertical columns. Greek architects built columns using a special technique called *entasis* to make them look straight, even though they were not.

Pillars of Society

The ancient Greeks were famous for their column building. Three styles of column were developed by Greek architects. Each column had three parts: the base, the shaft, and the capital. The Doric style was simple and had a plain capital. The Ionic column was narrower and had two scrolls on its capital. The Corinthian column was the most slender and had a more ornate capital. These column styles are still used today to decorate homes and offices.

capital

shaft

base

 Doric

 Ionic

 Corinthian

Epic Poetry

Stories about heroes and their deeds were told by ancient Greek poets in long poems called epics. Epic poems were **oral** at first and written down many years later. The most famous Greek epics, the *Iliad* and the *Odyssey* were composed by a blind poet named Homer around 700 B.C. The *Iliad* describes the long war between the Greeks and the people of Troy that began when a Trojan prince kidnapped the beautiful Greek queen, Helen. To get her back, the Greeks sent a large army, which included the Greek hero Achilles. After ten years of fighting, the Greeks rescued Helen and burned Troy to the ground. The *Odyssey* tells the story of Odysseus, a hero who spent ten years traveling home after the Trojan War. Along the way, Odysseus faced many terrible challenges, including a fight with a one-eyed creature called the Cyclops.

Great Playwrights

The ancient Greeks wrote many plays, some of which are still performed all around the world. The playwrights Aeschylus, Sophocles, and Euripides wrote tragedies. In tragedies, the main character faced challenges. A tragedy's ending was unhappy and the main character often died or was punished by the gods. Aristophanes wrote comedies. A comedy often poked fun at politics and people. It usually had a happy ending.

▲ *To win the Trojan War, the Greeks built a wooden horse and gave it to the Trojans as a gift. At night, Greek soldiers hiding inside the horse attacked Troy.*

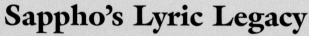

Sappho's Lyric Legacy

One of the few female poets of ancient Greece was Sappho, who lived sometime between 650 B.C. and 750 B.C. Sappho wrote poetry on the island of Lesbos. Until Sappho's time, poetry was mainly written from the point of view of the gods. Sappho changed this by writing poems about love and loss from her own point of view. Her poetry was written to be accompanied by a musical instrument called the lyre, which is why she is often called a lyric poet.

Theater

The ancient Greeks enjoyed both tragic and comic drama as far back as 500 B.C. Most cities had an open-air theater, or amphitheater, where plays were performed during the day. Some plays were put on as part of religious festivals honoring Dionysus, the god of wine and drama. Some festivals were competitions in which playwrights won a prize for the best play. At the beginning of a play, a chorus of actors stood in a circular area called the orchestra and sang or **recited** lines to the audience, describing what was taking place on stage. The chorus wore frowning, angry, smiling, or surprised masks to show their mood. Then, the actors were introduced. They spoke to the chorus. Only three men performed on stage but they played more than one part, including the female roles.

Dramatic Innovations

Amphitheaters, such as this one in Epidaurus, were designed to hold up to 14,000 people.

1. The chorus performed in the orchestra. The orchestra was 75 feet (23 meters) wide and was generally made of sand.

2. The auditorium, or seating area for people, was in two levels and formed a semi-circle around the orchestra.

3. The design of Greek amphitheaters was so good that even people in the back rows could see and hear perfectly.

4. After 300 B.C., the actors stood on a raised stage called a proskension. Behind the stage was the skene, where the actors changed costumes.

5. Actors entered and exited the stage through passageways at the sides called parados.

Alpha to Omega

Greek city-states were strong when they were united, but when they battled each other, they became vulnerable to outsiders. King Philip of Macedon ended these wars when he conquered Athens and Sparta in 338 B.C.

◀ *At the Battle of Marathon in 490 B.C., the Greek army fought the invading Persians. Even though they were outnumbered by the Persians, the Greeks won the battle and the Persians fled.*

The Persian Wars

By 500 B.C., the kingdom of Persia to the east of Greece had grown into a powerful empire. The Persians repeatedly attacked and conquered Greek colonies in Asia Minor and North Africa. In 490 B.C., the Persian ruler Darius I tried to attack the city of Athens. The Athenian and Persian armies fought a battle near the village of Marathon, north of Athens, which the Athenians won. In 480 B.C., the Persians attacked again with an army of 150,000 soldiers and 600 ships. Sparta's army led an **alliance** of 31 city-states against the invading Persians. The Persian navy was lured into a narrow channel off the island of Salamis in the Aegean Sea where their ships got trapped. The Greek ships were smaller and fitted with rams, which crushed their enemy's hulls. The Greek ships destroyed the Persian navy and the Persian army fled. The Persians never returned.

◄ Alexander the Great, seen at far left without a helmet, fights against King Darius of Persia, center, with his helmet on. Alexander had conquered most of the world by age 32.

The Peloponnesian War

After the Persian Wars, Athens organized another alliance of city-states, called the Delian League, to protect Greece from future Persian attacks. Since all the members of the alliance had to send **tribute** to Athens, the Athenians became very powerful. Sparta resented Athenian power and created an alliance of city-states to oppose Athens. In 459 B.C., Sparta and its allies defeated Athens in the first Peloponnesian War. Twenty-eight years later, the strong navy of Athens attacked Corinth, one of Sparta's allies. In response, Sparta began the second Peloponnesian War, which lasted until 404 B.C. Sparta eventually won the second Peloponnesian War when it built a navy to oppose Athens at sea. Sparta replaced Athenian democracy with an oligarchy.

Alexander the Great

By 338 B.C., King Philip of Macedon to the north of Greece had conquered Athens, Sparta, and most other Greek city-states. At age 20, his son Alexander expanded Philip's kingdom to include Egypt, India, and Persia. Alexander conquered many lands and became known as Alexander the Great. Many of the cities Alexander conquered were renamed after himself. Alexander thought highly of Greek culture and the Greek way of life. He settled Greeks in the conquered cities as a way to strengthen his control. The Macedonian conquest changed the Greek way of life, but it also preserved and spread Greek culture. This period in history is known as the Hellenistic Age because Alexander introduced Greek philosophy, language, art, and science to the captured cities.

◄ In about 350 B.C., Rome emerged as a power on the neighboring peninsula of Italy. Over time, the powerful army of Rome defeated its neighbors. By 146 B.C., all of ancient Greece was under Roman rule.

Glossary

alliance A partnership between peoples or countries

amphitheater A building with rows of seats rising gradually around an open stage or arena

artisan A person who has skill in making a particular product, such as pottery or jewelry

cavalry Soldiers who fight on horseback

colony An area controlled by a distant country

descended To come from ancestry or roots of a certain family or group

dialect A version of a language that is used in a particular part of a country

dowry The property that a woman brings to her husband in marriage

famine A great shortage of food that causes widespread hunger and starvation

flax A plant used to make linen, oil, and animal feed

fresco A kind of painting done on fresh moist plaster with colors dissolved in water

jury People who determine the outcome in a trial

legume Foods such as peas, beans, and lentils

mineral A natural, non-living substance

mosaic A decoration on a surface made by setting small colored pieces of glass or stone into another material to make pictures or patterns

oral Spoken or passed from person to person

ornate Decorated beautifully with great detail

patron Someone who supports or protects a city, nation, or people

peninsula A land mass that is surrounded on three sides by water

philosophy A set of beliefs about life and the world

plaster A paste of lime, water, and sand that hardens once dry and is used for coating walls and ceilings

random Not planned or having a set pattern

recite To repeat from memory or read aloud

replenish To refill

sanctuary A holy or sacred place

supernatural Beyond the usual powers of nature

terrace A raised bank of earth with sloping sides used for farming

terra cotta A hard baked clay used for pottery, statues, and building materials

tribute A payment made by one ruler or nation to another to show obedience or to obtain peace or protection

Trojan War A ten-year war between the ancient Greeks and Trojans in which the city of Troy was destoyed

utensil A tool, such as a fork, used to pick up food

Index

938
PEP

Peppas, Lynn.

Life in ancient
Greece.

10/69
6-14
5-16

DISCARD

BAKER & TAYLOR